Be Prepared To Get That Job

Nigel J. Copsey

Copyright ©2014 by Nigel J. Copsey.
All rights reserved.

This book or any portion thereof
may not be reproduced or used in any manner whatsoever
without the express written permission of the publisher
except for the use of brief quotations in a book review.

Dedication

To Tanya and Simon, who have used this process to good effect and thereby encouraged me to document it for others to try.

Contents

Introduction ix

1.0. But I don't know what kind of job I want 1

    1.1. Understanding some of our behavioural strengths 5

        Further insights into our behavioural preferences. 8

        The final analysis 10

My Notes. 12

2.0. Starting With The CV 13

    2.1. Points to consider when writing your CV 17

My Notes. 20

    3.0. Interview Preparation 21

    3.1. The Initial Steps 23

        Using the 'Web Site Menu' concept 25

    3.2. The Preparation Process: Mind-Mapping 28

        How we structure the "stories" 31

3.3. Weaknesses?...35

My Notes..37

4.0. Looking Forward..38

    4.1. In Conclusion 40

Bibliography & Recommended Reading...............41

About The Author – And His Other Books........43

BE PREPARED TO GET THAT JOB

Introduction

For most of us, job hunting can be a lonely and soul-destroying process, particularly if we have been made redundant through no fault of our own or if we are new to the job market and seeking our first job.

We have little to guide us. We have no way of knowing why an application or interview failed to land us the role. Where did we go wrong? Why weren't we selected?

After a few unsuccessful attempts, we begin to wonder what is wrong with us. We begin to doubt our own abilities. Self-confidence erodes to be steadily replaced by self-doubt.

What do we need to do to improve our chances of success when there is little or no feedback to guide us?

The purpose of this short booklet is to help you prepare both your CV and yourself in ways that increase your chances of obtaining a role you are more likely to enjoy and in which you will be more successful.

Over the past few decades I have had the good fortune of seeing both sides of the fence: helping candidates present themselves more effectively in both writing and in discussion; helping interviewers to understand what they should be looking for and how to find it by more effective questioning.

One thing I tell those who want to get a job is that the interviewer has an extremely difficult and responsible task. They have to understand the role and the strengths required to undertake it — in other words, what it takes for the incumbent to be a high performer. They then have to interview individuals in a way that helps them assess whether the person has those strengths in sufficient measure. Last but certainly not least, they have to make a decision that must be right not only for the company but also for the applicant. If the new recruit fails to deliver, there are negative consequences for the organisation and also for that recruit, who may well find him/herself suddenly back in the job market — perhaps with a perceived stigma of 'failure' attached.

This is what the interviewers are up against. They have a very difficult task to undertake. In fact, some are just as nervous as we are.

But they are not out to trip us up. They are not trying to judge whether we are a good person or a bad one.

They don't want to place someone into a role where they are likely to fail. They just want to ensure the person they select will be willing and able to do a great job for the company and for themselves.

My approach with the individual is therefore one of helping them to help the interviewer to clearly understand them, their strengths and weaknesses, enabling better chances of a right decision for all concerned.

So, if you are looking for techniques to "beat the interviewers at their own game", this book is not for you.

BE PREPARED TO GET THAT JOB

1.0. But I don't know what kind of job I want.

One problem many people mention when coming to me for help is that of not knowing what kind of job they want. This happens to not only the younger individuals finally exiting from their education but also to the more experienced ones.

Although this is a very important question, it is unfortunately not always an easy one for us to answer for ourselves.

I firmly believe in the eastern saying 'choose a job you really enjoy and you'll never do a hard day's work in your life.'

I have certainly found this to be a very true statement. When in my element, I put everything I have into what I'm doing, so much so that I am totally unaware of how much time is passing. These kinds of situation give me a buzz. I feel energised. It is only when it is all over that tiredness kicks in although it is a positive tiredness because of the sense of satisfaction that comes with it.

My book 'Lead To Win - *Pioneering Powerful Performance*', guides managers on ways to help their direct reports to achieve this state in the workplace. However, as a job seeker, the approach will be a different one for us.

My clients find it useful to utilise the process of Mind Mapping developed by Tony Buzan. We can map aspects of ourselves in order to understand our strengths and preferences to obtain an idea about what roles will give us more potential for enjoyment and success.

For this, we will need a large sheet of paper. A3 will be helpful but some people manage it across an A4 page or two. Alternatively, we can use a drawing, charting or even a Mind Mapping software program. Work with whatever suits you best, although you may find it better to start with pencil and paper to get used to the idea, then the transfer to the software package can be done as a part of the revision process.

In the centre of the paper, we write "ME" in block capitals and draw a circle or box around it.

ME

Some of the things we should include in our 'where I want to go' map are:

- Strengths
- Weaknesses
- Hobbies and interests
- Activities and 'subjects' I enjoy most
- And those I like least
- the things I do best

The Mind Map will start off looking something like this:

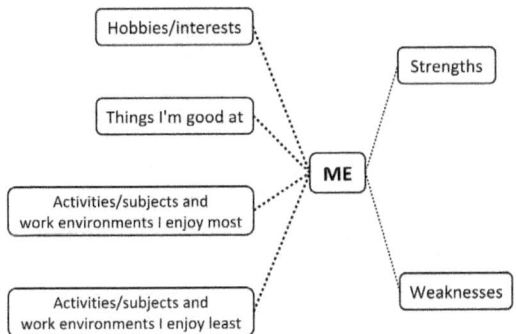

The next stage will be adding relevant boxes for each sub-item connected to each of these boxes in the same way as shown for the Strengths and Weaknesses in the following example.

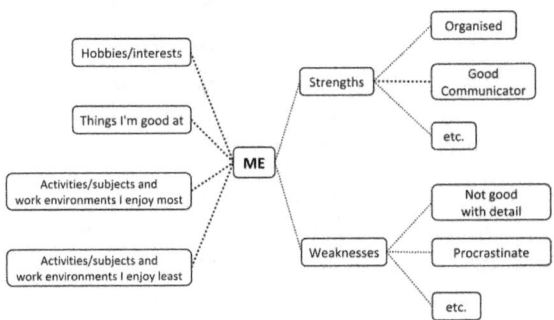

One of the nice things about using this method is that we rarely think in a straight line. For example, while we are putting a new item under "Activities/subjects I enjoy most", it may trigger in our mind a new item for "Activities/subjects I enjoy least". Thus, as our minds jump around, we have a framework on which to quickly record our thoughts in an organised way – and not forget them. It helps with the "flow".

If we have worked for a while, even as a part-timer, then we can also look back to identify the aspects we had found fulfilling in the roles we have had and, indeed, those parts we found boring or disliked doing.

The next stage is to study and analyse this information to better understand things like:

- the elements of the situations and activities we have enjoyed and done well
- those elements that made us dislike certain situations and activities and where we do not achieve as good a result.

Understanding our preferences more clearly in this manner can assist us to visualise what we need from a role and therefore give us more focus or direction in our search for one.

However, in order to do a much better job of it, we do need to dig deeper to bring an even more clear focus into our direction. Therefore, in the next section we will look at some other very important strengths that will help in this quest.

1.1. Understanding some of our behavioural strengths

Our behavioural strengths help determine what we are more likely to enjoy doing and potentially excel in. Choosing a role that calls for strengths contrary to ours is more likely to lead to discomfort because we are trying to be someone else all day, every day. This generally ends in dissatisfaction, lower performance and can even lead to stress.

I know this for a fact. I have been in a role that demanded almost totally opposite strengths to mine. After 18 months, I was very stressed and didn't know why I hated the job and was not performing as well as I normally did. Only after learning much later about the behavioural aspects of work did I very clearly understand what had gone wrong back then.

Don't let it happen to you!

To get an idea of where your strengths lie, take a look at the chart on page 7. There are four columns, each divided into two parts, "A" and "B".

There is no good or bad, right or wrong. We are merely seeking to understand ourselves. So, in each column, mark whether you are in the "A" segment or the "B" one.

You may find it difficult at times as an element of both "A" and "B" items may seem right for you or you are able to behave in both arenas. However, try to think about what comes easier or more naturally to you. The one you prefer. Which side you are more comfortable with.

One more point to be aware of. If you placed yourself in 1A, then it is likely that you are comfortable in 4B. Similarly, if you are in 1B, then you will probably be comfortable in 4A.

We will discuss these in a little more depth once you have determined your specific preferences.

My Behavioural Strengths

1	2	3	4
See the big picture Adventurous Like to take charge of people & situations	Enjoy socialising & making new friends Optimistic Warm hearted	Prefer to handle one thing at a time and complete it Spend time to get things right Calm in approach	Avoid risk-taking Obliging Very good with detail
Careful Moderate Helpful	Good at planning Need facts to analyse before deciding Think things through	Enjoy pressure/deadlines Energetic Enjoy plenty of variety	Prepared to take risks Autonomous, needing freedom to decide Ready to deal with opposition

You can now add these strengths to your mind map. Similarly, for things you realise you do not perform well at, you can place under the sub header of "Activities/subjects and work environments I enjoy least."

Further insights into our behavioural preferences.

Our behavioural preferences have a strong influence on our strengths and, by the same token, our weaknesses. They also play a large part in what we enjoy and fare well at and, of course, the reverse.

For example, if we are most comfortable handling one thing at a time and completing one task before moving to the next (3A), then we are likely to find ourselves uncomfortable working in a high-pressure multi-tasking role (3B).

Again, this is not to say we *cannot* do it. The majority of us can be flexible enough to cope with working on the other side of the fence, so to speak. However, the extent to which we can flex and for how long vary from person to person. Generally speaking, it is a case of coping with the uncomfortable to a degree, on occasion, when demanded.

Another way of looking at this is, so long as the job contains primarily things we enjoy, the odd bit of discomfort here and there is of little concern to us. We can cope with it.

In this context, one of the biggest selection

mistakes made by organisations is the placement of an individual into a role for which their behavioural strengths do not fit. This is often aided and abetted by individuals, who are not a right behavioural fit, applying for and going all out to get the job concerned.

This most often ends in disaster for both.

One prime example is that of a strong "technician" (e.g. accountant, programmer, engineer) being placed in a leadership role.

The reason for this is that the "technician" is so great at what they do because of their behavioural strengths, which are generally:

- 1B: Careful
- 2B: Planner
- 3A: Spends time to get things right first time
- 4A: Strong eye for detail, takes no risks

By stark contrast, a leader will have to be a person who:

- 1A: Likes to take charge of people and situations
- 2B: A planner. (One area of comfort.)
- 3B: Enjoy pressure deadlines and multi-tasking
- 4B: A risk taker, making decisions where there are no "rules", such as managing people.

One part of the problem is that there is a general perception that one is not successful unless one is climbing the managerial ladder. There is also the concern on the part of the organisation that a person be justly rewarded for their inputs.

It is true that a strong "technician" can lead a small technical team based on superior knowledge, but we must remember we are taking a person away from what they enjoy doing and are immensely successful at. In its stead, we are making them do many more things that are not at all satisfying for them.

I have noticed there is a small percentage of organisations that have two growth streams: one leadership oriented, the other being technical. This helps ensure the individual puts in more of what they enjoy which, for the "technician", is technological mastery at an even higher level.

The financial and status-oriented rewards are also in place to recognise the higher-level of value-add.

So, the moral of the story is that we should aim for what we are good at, and learn to deal with the small areas of discomfort in a more comfortable way.

The final analysis

In analysing the final mind map, it is helpful to consider two aspects: industry or profession and the type of role. The point I am aiming at here is that a specific role may be found in a number of different industries or professions.

One example that springs to mind is that of a PA. This means our search can be across a broader span of industries.

By contrast, our interests and strengths may point towards one particular industry, so our focus will therefore need to be more narrow.

Going through this exercise will not only make your direction more clear, it will also give a focus to what you put in your CV and, as we shall see later, what to include in your interview preparation.

My Notes.

2.0. Starting With The CV

Let's start at the beginning. We are unlikely to face an interviewer if we haven't applied for a job or if our CV contains no indications that we might well be not only the right fit for the role but also that we bring something extra to the equation.

Unfortunately, the majority of job applicants create CVs that are lacking as regards the latter point. These documents focus on the great favourites: skills, knowledge, experience and qualifications. Yes, these are important because the company will need someone with certain levels of these attributes. However, the professional interviewer will be looking for the 'icing on the cake' that spells out 'high performance'.

Let me give a live example.

> I was asked to help a young man, a qualified accountant, who had been made redundant from a large consultancy during an economic downturn.
>
> Apparently, for several months he had been frantically applying for jobs but gotten nowhere. The poor fellow was naturally not only depressed but also desperately anxious because he had a wife and child dependent upon him and a mortgage to meet payments upon.
>
> From what I understood, it was nothing to do with his performance or

lack thereof. The company was following the 'last in first out' method of selecting those who would be asked to leave. This is an accepted process to help ensure fairness as well as a sense of loyalty to their longer-term employees.

I agreed to meet with him and I requested him to bring a copy of his CV for me to review.

When we met, I glanced through his CV. I then looked him in the eye and tore up the document in front of him and tossed the pieces onto the table. You can imagine the startled look on his face as he asked me why on earth I had done that.

'Simple,' I replied. 'Tell me. How many other accountants might there be looking for employment in this huge city and who have very similar qualifications, responsibilities and experience as you have?'

'Hundreds,' he replied truthfully.

'Then why should I, as an employer, choose to select you rather than any other of the hundreds of accountants in Mumbai?'

'I don't know,' he replied, crestfallen and now even more concerned about his chances in the current market.

'Then please answer another question for me,' I continued. 'Tell me about a time when you went above and beyond the call of duty in order to satisfy a client.'

He thought for a moment and then related a situation where he really did put a lot extra into a project to help the client. I was genuinely staggered at the way he had dealt with a difficult situation.

'How did the client react?'

'They were extremely happy and even mentioned it to my boss.'

'So why isn't there any mention of this in your CV?' I asked.

'I didn't want to look as if I was bragging.'

Without further comment, I asked him for another example and he did so. Not as amazing as the first but nonetheless very impressive.

'So why isn't there any mention of this in your CV either?' I asked.

'Same reason as the first.'

'Speaking again as an employer, I would have no idea of how much you are willing to do to ensure my clients are satisfied, would I?'

'True.'

'So I could end up taking someone on who "just does a job" and offers little in the way of value-add for my business,' I added. 'Just because you think it's wrong to let me know about your approach?'

'I never thought about it that way,' he answered with a glimmer of realisation spreading steadily across his face.

'Then may I suggest you briefly mention these and any other significant achievements in a revised CV so people know what they are getting when they hire you?'

He agreed and he did revise his CV. Within a few weeks he had several job offers and has never looked back, I am pleased to say.

2.1. Points to consider when writing your CV

How often do we find out CV gets us nowhere in our attempt to get to interview stage?

Unfortunately, it can easily be because of the way we have presented ourselves rather than whether or not we are a strong candidate for the role advertised.

Think of the recruiter. It is a tough job trying to ensure they get the right person for a role. They have to make the unenviable decision that affects two parties — the organisation and the applicant. They neither want to hire a person that does not fit nor do they want to overlook a potential high performer.

In writing our CV, we must make it easier for them to make the right decision for us as well as the company, remembering we do not wish to be given a role in which we are likely to fail.

Very briefly, here are a few main points to consider when creating your CV.

- Be brief and to the point.

- List your various roles in reverse chronological order. (What you have been doing in the recent past will be more important to the company than what you did 10 or more years ago.)

- Avoid giving a long list of responsibilities. This tells the professional recruiter very little apart from the fact you may have had exposure to these aspects.

- Tailor the CV specifically for the role you are applying for. Don't just shoot off a standard CV to everyone.

- Consider having different versions specially tailored for the different kinds of jobs you want to apply for.

- Think about how many hundreds of other applicants have similar skills, knowledge, qualifications and experience, so include your more significant achievements so a potential employer can see what value-add you have created for others and which might well set you apart from other applicants.

- Give dates (minimum year & month) you moved from one company to another.

- Be honest in your statements. False claims have a habit of coming to the surface at some stage and can easily cause instant dismissal and/or complete lack of trust in you and your abilities/potential.

- Review it carefully to ensure clarity, there are no grammatical or spelling errors and the layout is easy on the eye.

When creating your CV, it can help if the contents are ordered as follows:

- Name and contact details.
- Very brief summary/overview of your more recent roles and your main strengths.
- Your roles, starting with the most recent: dates from-to, title, key responsibilities and significant achievements.
- Qualifications, awards, publications.
- A statement that references will be supplied upon request.

There is no need to add anything personal, such as marital status, hobbies, etc., unless they are pertinent to the job concerned.

My Notes.

3.0. Interview Preparation

I normally advise my clients to start working on this preparation as a part of preparing their CV. Because it is a relatively thorough exercise, it will provide important information that may well help the construction of the CV, not just for the interview.

It will be revised and improved perhaps more than once before it is ready and, on top of this, it is vital to practise speaking the prepared responses to be more certain and fluent when presenting them for real.

As one client said:

> 'My interview was last Wednesday and thank you for your advice with the mind maps. They really helped. I was able to answer all their questions and had a couple of examples for each competency which helped me relax during the interview.'

Feeling relaxed during the interview session is important because it allows you to give of your best.

Being ready with appropriate and truthful responses to the interviewer's questions also provides them with valuable information with which to make their decision about both your fit to the role and what you offer in terms of value-add.

You will also find the diagram you originally build will be revised and new aspects added as you face interviews for various roles. It is also something, like your CV, that will be updated as you move along your career path.

3.1. The Initial Steps

I mentioned a diagram and the client quote mentioned a mind map. Indeed, my experience has been that clients do find Tony Buzan's Mind Mapping approach straightforward and very relevant to what we need to achieve.

Let's take a look at what this involves for us.

We need to build a diagram or map that is concise and to the point. It helps us to be so during the interview, giving the interviewer as much valuable information as s/he needs within the time allotted. Long answers do not necessarily help, especially if they are topics of little interest to the interviewer.

Let me give another example.

> I was asked to help a man who was highly technical by nature and profession. I was told that, in spite of being called for many interviews, he had never been able to get beyond the first interview stage. He was coming to the end of a contract and it was imperative for him to find a new role, preferably a permanent one.
>
> On meeting this individual, I went through his CV. I was amazed at not only his qualifications but his added ability of speaking a number of languages. Not just the "usual" European ones. A couple of Nordic tongues were also included. I

honestly wondered why he had not been snapped up quickly by an organisation. Why was he not getting past the first hurdle?

To begin with, I thought it might be wise to just start an interview to see whether this would throw up some clues.

After telling him we were going to start an interview, I asked a question. He took quite some time to complete his answer, which he had given in fine detail. I asked another. He followed the same path of intricate detail and, after about 7-8 minutes, he suddenly stopped and looked perplexed.

'Er … I've forgotten what the question was,' he admitted.

'So have I. But I think I can see why you've been having the difficulty you have.'

Using the 'Web Site Menu' concept

Many people have found the use of this concept immensely helpful, especially if they tend towards the "information overload", often in an attempt to be helpful by giving as much detail as they can.

By contrast, we need to do two things initially:

- Give as little information as possible;
- Give the interviewer the information s/he really needs.

Sounds strange, doesn't it? Let me explain with an example.

Let's say the interviewer asks us what our three main strengths are. What we tend to do is give the first and then start to explain or illustrate it before moving on to the next, treating this too in the same manner before doing exactly the same with the third item.

This is all very well but ... is it of any interest to our listener? If not, we are wasting their time and the interviewer will be unable to cover all his/her important points in the time allotted for the meeting.

This is helpful to neither them nor us. We therefore need to approach this question differently and, to achieve much more, we use the '*Web Site Menu*' method.

Let's demonstrate:

'What are your three main strengths?'

- I'm organised in approach;
- a good communicator;
- and I'm decisive.

We stop there. Just like a menu on a Web page, we have given three options. Now it is open to the interviewer to select from this menu what s/he wants to understand more about. For example:

> 'Thank you. I would like to know about your communication abilities. Please tell me about them.'

We can now present another menu, like:

- I've had to make quite regular presentations;
- I generally work with others in a collaborative manner;
- I get along well with colleagues and other contacts from various parts of the world.

The next question we are asked will be aimed at drilling deeper into the area in which the interviewer has most interest and then we focus on giving concise information and an explanation about that.

The Web Site Menu really does help the interviewer get quickly to the things that matter. It gives them the control they require to guide us in that direction. It therefore follows that we are giving information the interviewer needs.

This is what I suggested to this person I was trying to help. Being in technology himself, the concept made a great deal of sense and we began working on it.

3.2. The Preparation Process: Mind-Mapping

In order to give these concise and helpful answers, we need to be prepared. We will now build the process for this based on the Mind Map concept.

In Chapter 1.0., we looked at the process of Mind Mapping aspects of ourselves in order to understand the kind of role that might suit us best. We can use the same process for understanding our strengths and preferences to obtain an idea about what roles will give us what we are likely to enjoy and be more successful at.

In fact, we can even use items from the same map because we will need to bring our strengths and weaknesses into our thinking process to help us find a direction.

In the centre of the paper, we write "ME" in block capitals and draw a circle or box around it.

What about me? What are my strengths? What are my weaknesses or, as they are often called "developmental areas"? What else defines what and who I am?

The next stage is to add these broad headings

as they occur to us. For example:

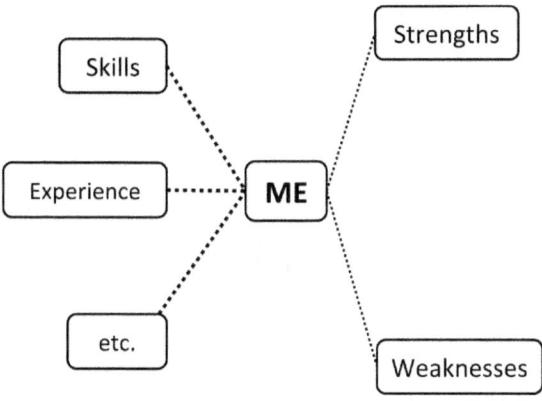

The nice thing about this method is that we can add more such items later in the process as we realise they are relevant. Meanwhile, the next step is to add sub-headings like the following:

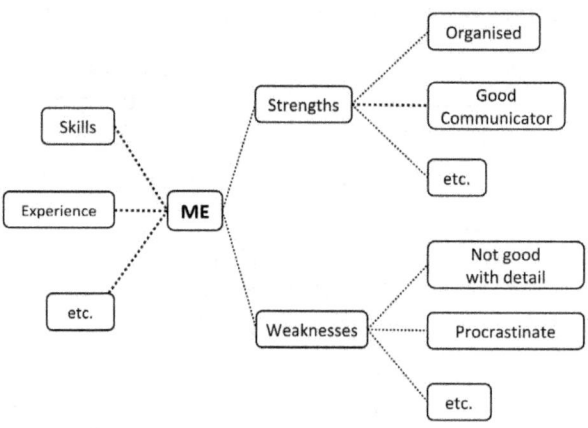

To keep the diagram small enough, the items on the left have not been broken into sub-heading lists, but these should also be expanded in the same manner. Again, on review, more can be added later.

Now comes the more difficult part. For each sub-heading (e.g. "Organised") we need some real illustrations of situations we have faced to be able to explain to the interviewer what we mean by the term. I will call them "Stories" but this by no means translates into "fairy stories"! We need truthful accounts.

How we structure the "stories"

Well, we need to keep them brief and to the point. Yet, at the same time, they must illustrate what we mean by "Organised". There are four crucial elements to use:

- **Situation:** briefly, in one or two sentences, we describe the situation we faced.
- **Implications:** again briefly, what was the situation costing, preventing, causing, or what were the potential risks involved?
- **Action:** briefly, the action we took to solve the problem, put things right.
- **Result:** briefly, what did we achieve? The cost savings, greater throughput, extent to which the situation was eased?

Again, I stress, just one or two sentences for each. If the interviewer needs more, s/he will ask for it.

Do you remember the case of the gentleman who put everything forward in great depth and detail from question one? He took this idea on board and after several sessions, he had mastered the approach. His answers were brief, concise, helpful and to the point. I would also like to add that he too got several job offers from which he was able to choose what suited him and his family the best.

In other words, it works!

A Few More Important Points

When building the Mind Map, merely jot a key word or two for each element of the story as reminders. These will help you recount the story when practising. It also prevents too much overcrowding of the diagram. If you are concerned about remembering the sentences, then by all means have a separate sheet with the punchy sentences written down for reference.

Interviews tend to cover a number of things and, therefore, a story that we might have prepared for "Organised" may be useful to illustrate something else. This leaves us in a dilemma should the interviewer want to dig into "Organised" later in the conversation. How do we deal with this situation?

The implications are that we are at a loss, which can lead to us losing composure, which can make us less effective in getting beyond the current interview. It may also make the interviewer less certain about whether that strength was real or made up. Again, will that knock us out of the running?

The action I normally recommend rather strongly is that two or three illustrations from our past experiences should be prepared for each of the items. Three is preferable.

What is the likely result? Well, on "losing" the story on "Organised", we can now say something like 'The situation I described earlier regarding … also relates to this. (Think for a moment.) Another situation that comes to mind is when …'

Having three can also mean we will remember one or two if we have practised thoroughly, whereas if we only have one and cannot recall it in the heat of the moment, we are stuck. We are also covered should the interviewer respond by requesting another example in order to understand more clearly.

Thus, our preparation will be a fuller version of this kind of picture, as illustrated on the next page.

Another nice thing about Mind Maps is the fact that it can also aid the recall process. We tend to visually follow the links in our mind.

BE PREPARED TO GET THAT JOB

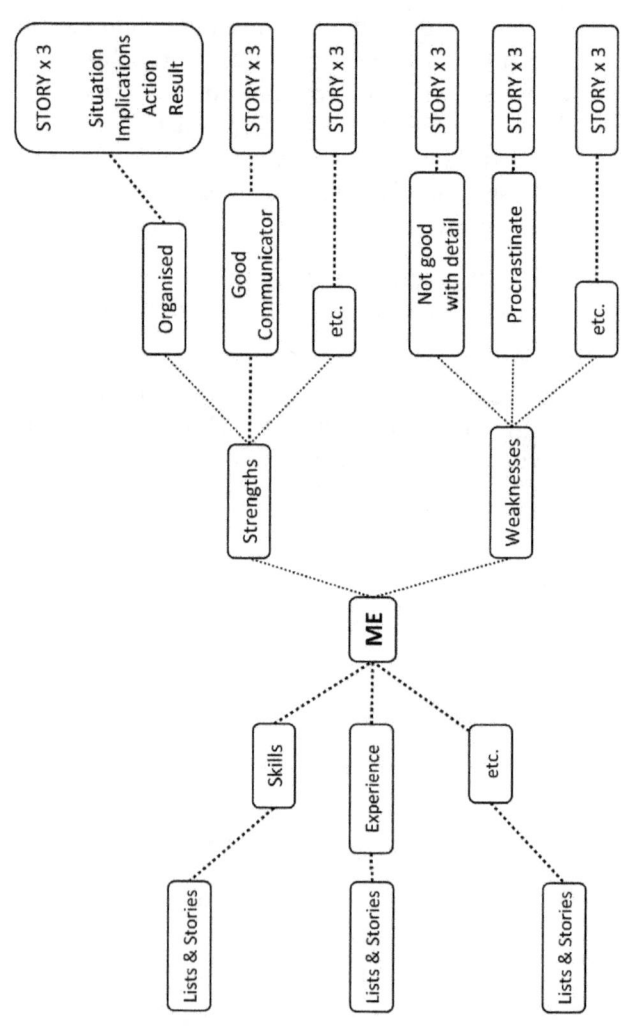

3.3. Weaknesses?

Should we admit to having a weakness, let alone three?

It's a sad fact of life. None of us is perfect. We all have weaknesses. Some are by virtue of the strengths we have. In other words, because we are, for example, great with detail, we are likely to find it more difficult to see the "big picture". The reverse will also be likely to apply if we are a "big picture" person.

We should not hesitate to note down our biggest developmental areas. However, if we are aware of them thanks to the fact they let us down on occasion, what have we done to prevent it happening too often or too badly? You cannot always get rid of a weakness but it is possible to manage it on occasion, when needed.

That may give you food for thought. What does let you down more than you would like? Working with managers as their coach, I often find they can, after thought and reflection, pinpoint something that tells them that things are beginning to happen inside them. Identifying this enables them to use this feeling as a "trigger". In other words, a warning that things could go wrong unless they manage the situation differently to their natural response to it.

The supporting aspect is creating an action, a way of handling things more effectively than they would under normal circumstances. The trigger is now a prompt to follow this action.

Another approach is that, by understanding our limitations, we focus on ensuring we reduce the possibility of them happening. An example I use when training or coaching managers is my own limitation. Quite honestly, I am someone who has great difficulty with detailed stuff. I get lost in it or go to sleep mentally when being bombarded with it. So, when it comes to completing my accounts, I know that if I spend any more than an hour on this fine detail and preciseness, I begin to lose my cool and get terribly stressed out!

The solution I found is to limit the time I spend on this laborious task. I set the clock to sound the alarm within 45 minutes of starting. When the alarm goes off, I stop working on the accounts and turn to something I enjoy much more. I go back to them later but again, no more that 45 minutes. This allows me to get the detailed work done in smaller chunks and thereby keep my sanity!

No, I am not straying from the point. What I am driving towards is the fact that we can admit to a weakness and also speak about what we do to limit its negative impact. Again, we illustrate with an example from our lives, as I have just done but in short, crisp and more precise sentences than the ones I have used! We talk about the Situation, its Implications, the Action we took, and the Results.

My Notes.

4.0. Looking Forward

Your CV and, indeed, your Mind Map, should not be static documents. My advice is to keep both updated on a fairly regular basis. I used to keep a notepad in the top drawer of my desk and, each time I achieved something, I would note it down on the notepad. In fact, a suggestion I make in my book "Lead To Win — *Pioneering Powerful Performance*" fits comfortably with this idea.

> "It is important to quantify/qualify the improvements gained from an activity, particularly in an operations or back-room function, because whilst in the thick of things we begin to wonder if we have made any progress, made a difference, to our area of responsibility. There is always something demanding a fix, so we only see the problems rather than celebrate the successes. I have certainly experienced this, more than just a few times! Reviewing the achievements is a refreshing experience and brings back the positivity into our demeanour, I promise you."

Reviewing this list, especially when we change roles (even internally) gives us the opportunity to add an item or a summary of similar achievements to our Mind Map notes, including the brief story while it is fresh in our mind.

Keeping up this practice ensures our CVs are

up date and we are well-stocked with useful stories in readiness for the next job-hunt and the interviews that go with it.

4.1. In Conclusion

A suggestion I made to my own children is: treat job hunting as a full-time occupation and practise your interview responses regularly so you are mentally prepared, even at short notice, to face the event. It will help lessen the nervousness when you are in front of the recruiter. It will help you create your own luck.

If you are seeking a management/leadership role and obtain it, you will probably find my earlier book "Lead To Win – *Pioneering Powerful Performance*" a strong guide to achieving great results with your team.

Finally, my best wishes to you in landing a job you really enjoy and become successful in!

Bibliography & Recommended Reading

Tony Buzan with Barry Buzan: "The Mind Map Book". BBC Books ISBN 0 563 37101 3

Ken Robinson: "Finding Your Element". Allen Lane ISBN 978 1 846 14416 5

BE PREPARED TO GET THAT JOB

About The Author – And His Other Books

Nigel J. Copsey has decades of results-oriented experience in managing, training, consulting and coaching in a number of countries and even in unusual situations.

During his career he has focused strongly upon performance improvement, rarely accepting the *status quo*. This resulted in a great deal of study, observation and experiment that, together with the many mistakes he made, taught him a great deal.

In this book, he shares some of his learning from the area of recruitment — particularly in helping job hunters be more successful in obtaining a role which they can enjoy and be successful at.

Nigel's other books:

Non-Fiction - Management.

"Lead To Win — Pioneering Powerful Performance". (Leadership) ISBN 9781489556615

(Available from Amazon in many countries in both print and Kindle formats.)

www.ingramcontent.com/pod-product-compliance
Lightning Source LLC
Chambersburg PA
CBHW051821170526
45167CB00005B/2107